T0348194

ALPINE AUSTRALIA

Mt Twynam - Main Range, New South Wales. *CL*

This book is for my grandchildren, Kallen and Olivia - may we have many exciting adventures together, exploring these magestic mountains and enjoying everything that they offer.

- CRAIG -

For my wonderful mum, Margaret Munn, whose unconditional love and encouragement was boundless.

- CHRIS -

ALPINE AUSTRALIA

A CELEBRATION OF THE AUSTRALIAN ALPS

CRAIG LEWIS AND CHRIS MUNN

BOILING BILLY
PUBLICATIONS

Sunset over The Paralyser and Mount Anton, New South Wales. *CL*

Alpine: pertaining to any part of a lofty mountain; very high or elevated; or a part of the Alps.

Survivors - Snow gums along McKay Road, Falls Creek - Victoria. *CM*

THE AUSTRALIAN ALPS

CONTENTS

"Conspicuously elevated above all heights . . . and swollen by many rugged protuberances, the snowy and craggy sienitic cone of Mount Kosciuszko is seen cresting the Australian Alps in all the sublimity of mountain scenery."

Paul Edmund Strzelecki

INTRODUCTION

Australia's Alpine regions are places of extremes. During winter they are often covered in a metre or more of snow where ferocious blizzards can rage for days on end as cold fronts push in from the west and south. Clouds roll in obscuring the ranges, creating 'white-outs' which can restrict visibility to only a few metres. It is often these unyielding conditions which shape the snow-covered landscape into a thing of immense beauty. This is the Australian Alps in all her crowning glory when she wears her snowy mantle.

On a broad scale the Australian Alps is seen as the mountainous area stretching between Canberra in the north to the outskirts of Melbourne in the south. We have however, narrowed the scope for this book to the elevated parts of New South Wales' Snowy Mountains, home to some of our highest mountains, including our highest, the 2228 metre Mount Kosciuszko, and in Victoria to the areas of Mount Bogong, at 1986 metres is that state's highest peak, and nearby Mount Hotham and Mount Buller/Stirling. It is these snow-covered winter landscapes which we have focused our lenses on for Alpine Australia.

But first, a little history about the Alps. Long before the coming of Europeans, the traditional owners moved into the Alpine regions during the summer months. It is estimated that they have been regular visitors to these higher parts for more than 5000 years. Here they performed ceremonial tasks and feasted on bogong moths - the plump insects migrate to the cool alpine peaks over summer. But by the mid-1800s European influences in the area had all but pushed the first people out of the mountains. It's ironic that Aboriginal guides where used by early explorers to show the traditional mountain pathways.

Explorers Hume and Hovell sighted the Snowy Mountains on their trek from Lake George to Corio Bay in 1824. Others followed, pushing further into the mountains. In February 1840 Stewart Ryrie ascended the Rams Head Range and a month later Polish scientist Paul Edmund Strzelecki reached the summit of Australia's highest peak, naming it in honour of another Pole, Tadeusz Kościuszko. Surveyors and scientists then began making their way to the Snowy Mountains, mapping the region and naming many of its features.

In Victoria, botanist Baron Ferdinand von Mueller and explorers Angus McMillan and Alfred Howitt pushed into the valleys and mountains. Von Mueller's botanical discoveries were the result of five journeys through the Victorian Alps and Southern New South Wales during the 1850s.

During the 1850s and 1860s gold discoveries saw prospectors penetrate deep into the mountains in search of the precious metal. The now ghost town of Kiandra is just one stark reminder of the hardships faced by these prospectors.

Around the 1820s graziers began to exploit the high plains, pushing stock onto the sweet grasses of the alpine meadows. The practice continued until 1958 when grazing leases were abolished in the then Kosciusko State Park, now Kosciuszko National Park. In Victoria, alpine grazing continued in an ad-hoc fashion until it was finally abolished from the alpine areas in 2014.

But debate still runs hot with regards to the presence of large numbers of feral horses in alpine national parks on both sides of the border. In summer it's not uncommon to see mobs of brumbies grazing in parts of the Rams Head Range in the shadow of Mount Kosciuszko. One side of the argument says the brumbies are part of our folklore and heritage and the horses should remain in the mountains. The other camp pushes the environmental impacts of these hard-hoofed animals on the fragile and sensitive alpine landscape. In 2018 the New South Wales Government passed a bill to protect brumbies from being culled in Kosciuszko National Park.

In the early 1900s recreational skiing started to gain popularity in the Snowy Mountains, most notably in the Perisher Valley. Accommodation venues were constructed as people came to the mountains to discover its snowy delights. But well before this, back in the 1860s gold miners at Kiandra started a ski club and ran downhill skiing competitions. Using hand fashioned wooden skis, competitors would go headlong downhill, using a stick of wood as a brake to slow themselves. In Victoria, skiing began at Mount Buffalo in the 1890s with the Mount Buffalo Chalet constructed in 1910. Mount Buffalo was also the site of Australia's first ski tow which was constructed in 1936. Today New South Wales boasts seven lifted resorts while Victoria has five.

Next came the engineering marvel which is the Snowy Mountains Scheme. Commencing shortly after World War II, the scheme's network of dams and tunnels captures and then diverts water and snowmelt through hydro-electric power stations before being offered up for irrigation use along the Murrumbidgee and Murray River systems. In Victoria the Kiewa Hydroelectric Scheme, which commenced construction at the end of the 1930s, is centred on Falls Creek. It is the second largest hydro power generator on the mainland after the Snowy Mountains Scheme.

A side benefit of the Snowy Mountains Scheme is the network of roads and tracks constructed during its development, which in turn, helped open up the area for visitors.

What of my long-term affinity with the mountains? Like many who come to the area, my early visits were in winter where I discovered the thrills, and sometimes spills, of downhill skiing. Living at the time in Newcastle, these excursions

became much anticipated annual events with my then young son and friends. In the beginning it was with my 'trainer wheels' firmly attached, learning to ski on the gentle terrain of Mount Selwyn. As skills and confidence improved it was time to branch out and experience the steeper slopes and more advanced runs of the various other Snowy Mountains resorts. My son, who is now in his thirties, first clipped on a pair of skis just after his third birthday. My grandson has just done the same. And Mount Selwyn, the friendly little resort which gave me my first taste of mountain magic, still holds a prominent place in my snow-filled winter experiences.

But what were the mountains like in the summer with nary a skerrick of snow to be seen? I had to find out. Standing on the summit of Australia's highest peak soon went from being a dream to a reality. Exploring the Main Range on the well-trodden Main Range Walking Track took me to our loftiest mountains, and all of this within the bounds of a day walk. This only whetted my appetite to venture further into the mountains, to see what was over the next ridge and to follow the valleys. This goal however, required donning a backpack and heading off into the wilderness. Mount Jagungal beckoned as did The Kerries and Brassy Mountains, The Pilot Wilderness and Tin Mines were also on my radar and were

---

An early winter blizzard had swept across the Snowy Mountains, bringing much excitement for the snow season ahead. After the front had moved off towards the east and the skies cleared, I enjoyed a magic afternoon exploring the first of the season's snowfalls around Guthega Trig. A day or two of warm weather followed by overnight freezes had created some intricate ice sculptures. CL

soon explored. Across the border Mount Bogong and the Bogong High Plains cast their spell and before long I was enjoying their hidden secrets.

Summer four-wheel drive trips offered more opportunities which took me into the heart of the Victorian High Country and around the fringes of the Snowy Mountains.

Long term outback travel then started to consume my winters as I travelled to these remote areas on writing and photographic assignments. Too hot in summer, it was the winters when journeys to the vast inland and deserts were most practical. During this time my winter sojourns to the mountains became few and far between.

Fast forward almost a decade and now I'm firmly ensconced on the edge of the mountains. A visit to the mountains is now literally only a hop, skip and a jump! Cross-country skis and snowshoes have, for the most part, replaced the downhill gear; crowded resorts and lift queues have been replaced by the solitude of the backcountry and the high, snow covered peaks offer both a challenge and a sense of achievement.

I first met fellow photographer Chris Munn a few years ago while photographing the iconic Craigs Hut in the Victorian High Country. I was there making images for a book on the High Country's classic mountain huts. Chris was shooting images for his online gallery. While waiting for the best light we got chatting about our mutual affections for the mountains; mine biased towards the New South Wales' 'Snowy's' and his heavily weighted to the Victorian Alps,

which is easily accessed from his home base in the picture postcard village of Yackandandah. A year later I hatched the idea for this book, which then incubated for another year, in between other writing and photography projects.

When I eventually got around to planning this project my instinct told me Chris would be the ideal collaborator for this book. His affinity with the Victorian Alps has very much shone through with his inspiring images and words.

One thing is for sure, after the lure of the Australia Alps has taken hold; its enchanting winter landscapes will draw you in, urging you back time and time again to experience its many wonders and beauties.

- CRAIG LEWIS -

KYBEYAN, NEW SOUTH WALES 2018

SUNSET ON THE HORN - MT BUFFALO, VICTORIA. *CM*

Boulder fields on the Rams Head Range, New South Wales. *CL*

ALPINE AUSTRALIA
NEW SOUTH WALES

MOUNT KOSCIUSZKO
&
THE MAIN RANGE

AUSTRALIA'S HIGHEST MOUNTAIN, THE 2228 METRE HIGH MOUNT KOSCIUSZKO, IS THE CROWNING JEWEL OF THE MAIN RANGE. HOSTING ALL BUT ONE OF MAINLAND AUSTRALIA'S 2000 METRE PLUS HIGH PEAKS, INCLUDING MOUNT TOWNSEND (2210 METRES), CARRUTHERS PEAK (2145 METRES), MOUNT TWYNAM (2196 METRES) AND MOUNT TATE (2068 METRES), THE MAIN RANGE, WHICH IS CLOAKED IN A MANTLE OF SNOW FOR MUCH OF THE YEAR, STRETCHES IN A GENTLE ARC FROM THE RAMS HEAD IN THE SOUTH TO CONSETT STEPHEN PASS AND THE ROLLING GROUNDS IN THE NORTH. IT IS PART OF THE GREAT DIVIDING RANGE AND OFFERS THE ONLY EVIDENCE OF GLACIAL ACTIVITY ON THE MAINLAND,

MOUNT KOSCIUSZKO

On the afternoon of March 12th, 1840 Polish born geologist and explorer Paul Edmund Strzelecki ascended the summit of Australia's highest mountain, which he named in honour of a compatriot, the freedom fighter, General Tadeusz Kościuszko. Rising to a height of 2228 metres, Mount Kosciuszko attracts over 30 000 visitors each year, with most climbing the mountain during the summer months.

The ice encrusted rock cairn marks the summit of Mount Kosciuszko. On a fine day–which we fortunately encountered on this mid-winter visit–the views from the summit offer sweeping vistas out across the Main Range. CL

Mount Kosciuszko looms large on the western skyline on the
southern approach from Etheridge Gap.

The Abbott Range with the peak of Mount Townsend at the back. At 2209 metres, Mount Townsend is a mere 19 metres lower than Mount Kosciuszko and is Australia's second highest mountain. It is named after the then Assistant Surveyor General, Thomas Scott Townsend who undertook an extensive survey of the Main Range in the summer of 1847.

The ice sculptured summit cairn marks mainland Australia's highest point. Rarely visited in winter, the windswept peak can be shrouded in cloud and fog for days on end, with white-out conditions requiring experienced navigation skills. But on fine days the spectacle which unfolds from the summit is nothing short of breathtaking.

THE ALPINE PEAKS

VIEW FROM MOUNT KOSCIUSZKO

Looking north from the summit of Mount Kosciuszko, the highest peaks of the Main Range are laid out before you. Off to the left are Abbotts Peak, Mount Townsend and Muellers Peak, while dominating the middle foreground is Mount Northcote and Mount Clarke. Tucked in behind is Mount Lee, Carruthers Peak and Mount Twynam, and at 2196 metres is mainland Australia's third highest mountain. To the right is the headwaters of the Snowy River.

THE COOTAPATAMBA CORNICE

The impressive Cootapatamba Cornice forms on the south side
of Mount Kosciuszko during winter and lasts as a snow drift
well into summer. Cornices are formed when windblown snow
creates a ledge where there is a sharp variation in terrain,
such as a mountain peak or steep ridge. The Cootapatamba
Cornice forms on the Kosciuszko South Ridge above the glacial
Lake Cootapatamba.

MAIN RANGE

VIEW OF THE MAIN RANGE FROM PORCUPINE ROCKS

Formed some 500 million years ago, the Main Range is mainland Australia's only true alpine environment. It was once laying on the floor of an ancient ocean but over time movements of the earth's crust caused folding, fracturing and uplifting until some 200 million years ago when the range and surrounding land raised out of the ocean. Over the ensuing millennia the softer rock has been eroded by wind, rain and frosts, as well as glacial action during the last ice age. This view from Porcupine Rocks shows the sweeping arc of the Main Range, including the high peaks of mounts Kosciuszko, Townsend and Tywnam.

Sunset on the Main Range (from left) Little Twynam, Mount Twynam, Mount Anton and Mount Anderson

Winter on the Main Range is a place of extremes. Above the treeline, which is around 1800 metres, you are exposed to the full force of the elements. Here blizzards can rage for days on end as cold fronts sweep in from the west. Another feature

are 'white-outs'. These occur when cloud rolls in obscuring visability to a little more than being able to see your hand in front of your face! Winter trips on the Main Range are not to be undertaken lightly. Even day trips need a high level of preparation. But for those wanting to explore these snow covered parts of the ranges, the rewards are well worth the effort.

Day trippers can visit the areas around The Rams Head from the top of the Kosciuszko Express chairlift from Thredbo. This is also a good staging point for an assult of the Mount Kosciuszko

Taking in the sweeping vistas from Mount Kosciuszko. When the weather is clear there are uninterrupted panoramas across to the Victorian Alps in the west while to the north the peaks of the Main Range dominate the skyline. In the wide valley below the fledgling Snow River starts its run to the ocean.

RIGHT: Exploring the Main Range during winter is only for those who are well prepared, as well as keeping a keen eye on the weather.

summit. Accessing the Main Range from Charlotte Pass offers opportunities to trek up the Old Summit Road via Seamans Hut to Kosciuszko summit, or branch out towards the Blue Lake area and Carruthers Peak. From Guthega there are routes onto the northern parts of the Main Range via the Snowy River at Illawong and onto the area around Mount Twynam; while a jaunt from Guthega up to Guthega Trig and a ciruit around Consett Stephen Pass will lead you onto Mount Tate and the Tate East Ridge.

A good option for the less experienced is to visit with one of the many experienced guide operators who offer day and longer jaunts into the ranges.

The steep precipices of The Sentinel and Watsons Crags fall away sharply into the Western Fall of the Main Range and are in stark contrast to the relatively gentle terrain of the Main Range's eastern slopes. The imposing bulk of Mount Jagungal rises in the background.

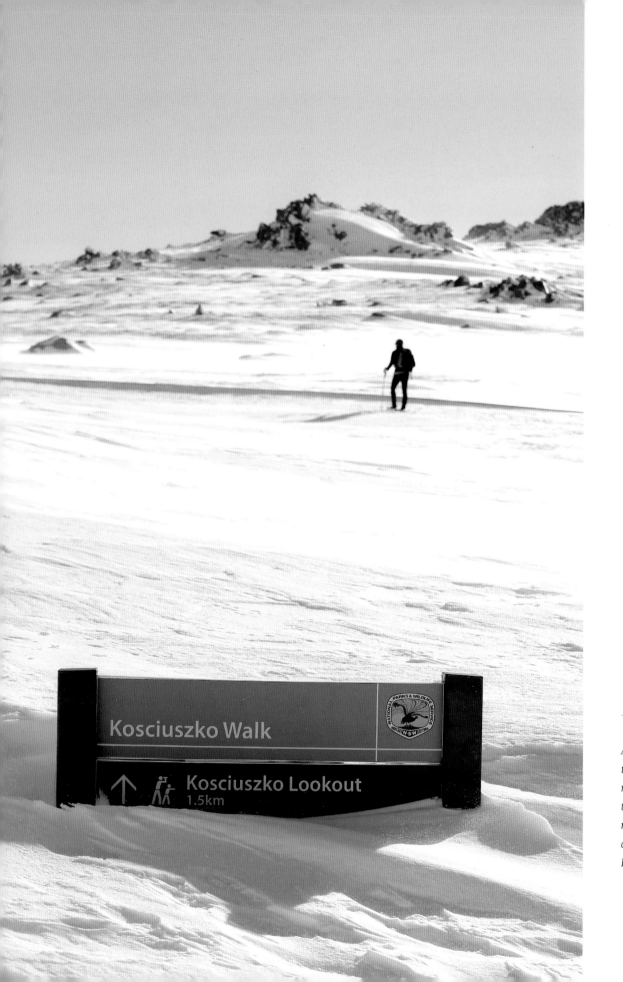

A snowshoe trip to Mount Kosciuszko and the Main Range is a highlight of our winter mountain adventures, but the trek really has to be planned around good weather. There are no snow poles to follow in winter. The most direct route is from the top of the Kosciuszko Express chairlift at Thredbo. CL

KOSCIUSZKO WALK

One of Australia's iconic day walks, the 13km return summer ramble from Eagles Nest at the top of Thredbo to the summit of Australia's highest peak is undertaken by an average 30 000 people each year. In summer it's a pretty sedate walk following, for the most part, a steel mesh walkway. The journey can also be undertaken from Charlotte Pass and is slightly longer at 19km return.

However, with winter snowfalls it becomes a much more serious undertaking. Whether tackling the summit on showshoes or cross-country skis you will need to be well prepared for the extreme alpine environment and often changable weather conditions. For the inexperienced wanting to make the winter ascent there are a number of tour operators offering guided day trips. No matter which way you go, it is a truly amazing experience to be standing on the roof of Australia.

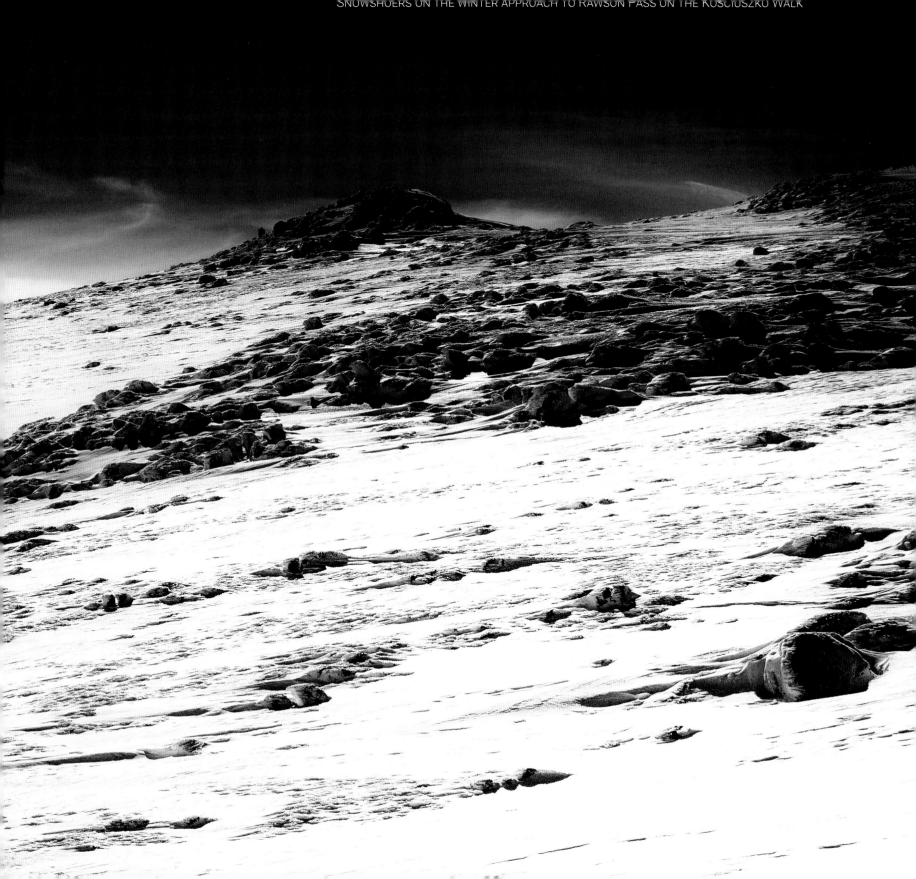

COOTAPATAMBA HUT

Cootapatamba Hut is a former stream-flow gauging station built by the Snowy Mountains Authority. The bright red hut, at a minuscule 2.5 metres by 2.5 metres, is now an emergency shelter; and along with Seamans Hut, is only one of two shelter huts on the Main Range. Located on a flat beside Swampy Plain River and below Lake Cootapatamba, the hut is within easy striking distance from Mount Kosciuszko. The weatherboard structure features a unique chimney-like roof access for times of snow build-up.

Beacon like in its striking red guise, Cootapatamba Hut has acted as a refuge from the vagaries of the alpine weather since its construction in the 1950s.

47

THE RAMS HEAD RANGE

The jumbled assortment of rocky granite tors and crags of the Rams Head Range are the result of weathering by water and ice. There are three 2000 metre plus peaks in the group – the central apex is known as The Rams Head (2193m) with North Rams Head (2178m) and South Rams Head (2053m) other prominent features. Stewart Ryrie was the first European to ascend this range on 15 February 1840, just one month before Strzelecki.

This confused array of boulders, some seemingly placed atop one another, feature throughout the Rams Head Range. Summer sees the range carpeted with snowgrass and a profusion of alpine wildflowers while winter tranforms the area into a pristine snowscape.

A snowshoer approaching North Rams Head (2178m) after ascending the range from the Swampy Plain River valley below Lake Cootapatamba.

Juxtaposed against the stark white snowscape, this weathered rocky outcrop is just one of numerous protuberances which make up the boulder field of the Rams Head Range. Being close to Thredbo Top Station, the range is a popular day destination, both summer and winter.

THE WESTERN FALL

The western fall of the Main Range boasts the steepest parts of the entire Snowy Mountains. Looking towards the range from the west, the imposing sentinels of Mount Townsend and Abbott Peak obscure the presence of Mount Kosciuszko, just as it had done when Hume and Hovell glimpsed the snow covered peaks in 1824 from near present day Tumbarumba. In 1840 Strzelecki's party came at the range from the west via the Geehi Valley and Hannels Spur–the towering, rocky peaks offering a breathtaking backdrop.

LEFT: The steep ascent from the Geehi Valley to the ramparts of the Main Range offered up challenges to the early explorers. Today, experienced walkers can follow in the footsteps of Strzelecki by trekking up Hannels Spur from the picturesque Geehi Valley.

Unlike the often parched Monaro Plains to the east, the western side of the Main Range captures the strong westerly air stream, where in winter, it rises abruptly from the south-west slopes, the moisture-laden clouds depositing their bounty as snow on the high peaks. This in turn allows tall mountain ash forest to thrive in the moist, protected gullies lower down.

The stunning panorama which is laid out from Scammells Ridge Lookout on The Alpine Way. Author Elyne Mitchell wrote of the Main Range's Western Face '...the mystery of deep gullies, the wonderful steepness of snow faces and tumbling ridges... The western face had the magnificence of all great mountains...'

Some 20 000 years before the European explorers, indigenous tribes made their annual summer pilgrimage to the mountain range, feasting on bogong moths and participating in rituals. Although the tribes have long since made their last descent into the valleys below, one can easily visualise the groups as they enjoyed the view from these highlands. According to author Alan E J Andrews, '... there is no Aboriginal name associated with our highest peak, despite that Spencer of Waste Point may have claimed that our Mt Townsend could have been associated with the Targangil sound'.

The jagged ridges of Watsons Crags and The Sentinel rise sharply to the skyline. Seen here from Scammels Ridge Lookout on the Alpine Way, the snow laden clouds, whipped in by another approaching cold front, obscure the loftiest peaks with a protective mantle, their intensity adding a dramatic feel to the end of the day as the sun sinks behind the western horizon. CL

KOSCIUSZKO NATIONAL PARK

Characterised by rugged mountains and boasting an alpine climate, where much of the higher ground can be covered by a metre or more of snow each winter, the vast 6900-square-kilometre Kosciuszko National Park is home to mainland Australia's highest peak, Mount Kosciuszko, for which the park is named. Stretching from the Victorian border in the south to near Tumut in the north, the park is the source of the fledgling Snowy River, the Murray River and Gungarlin River. The park came into existence in the mid 1940s, becoming the Kosciusko State Park in 1944 and then proclaimed as Kosciuszko National Park in 1967.

View from Mount Perisher - Kosciuszko National Park
A late afternoon jaunt found me on the western flanks of Mount Perisher, just outside the resort boundary. As the sun made its early mid-winter descent, it lit up the landscape with shades of yellow, blue and purple. Off in the distance the never-ending vistas of the Main Range offered a rollercoaster journey across some of the country's highest peaks. CL

PERISHER
&
SURROUNDS

HOME TO AUSTRALIA'S MOST POPULAR SKI RESORT, THE PERISHER VALLEY IS A MECCA FOR DOWNHILL SKIERS. ORIGINALLY USED BY EARLY GRAZIERS AS PART OF SUMMER SNOW LEASES, MANY OF THE AREA'S PROMINENT LANDMARKS, INCLUDING PERISHER, THE PARALYSER AND BLUE COW HAVE BEEN BESTOWED THEIR UNIQUE NAMES BY THESE EARLY PIONEERS. RECREATIONALLY, THE PERISHER VALLEY DEVELOPED WITH THE POPULARITY OF SKIING IN THE EARLY PART OF THE 1900S, WITH THE ORIGINAL KOSCIUSKO HOTEL BEING THE FIRST ACCOMMODATION FACILITY TO BE CONSTRUCTED IN THE MOUNTAINS.

Late afternoon on Mount Perisher looking towards Betts Camp. When the wind is howling around the peaks the string of protected valleys, which stretch from Perisher to Charlotte Pass, offer a much more pleasant destination for backcountry explorers on cross-country skis or snowshoes.

Looking towards the Perisher Range from Blue Calf Mountain. As the weather rolled in from the west, the last rays of sun penetrated gaps in the cloud blanket as the inky darkness descended, lighting this rocky outcrop below Mount Perisher with a warming glow.

Sunset over Blue Calf Mountain. The mountain is the home of the final station on the Skitube train which runs from Bullocks Flat via Perisher Valley and offers a great viewpoint to many of the Main Range's highest peaks, including Mount Kosciuszko.

THE PARALYSER

James Spencer is commonly referenced to have named Perisher and The Paralyser. Spencer, a local pastoralist and mountain guide from Waste Point, held grazing leases on much of the Main Range. Folklore suggests that when mustering his stock in the face of a blizzard, he is purported to have said of the conditions 'This is truly a perisher!' when on the range at Mt Perisher. Sometime later, when on the peak to the west, Spencer is believed to have said 'If that was a perisher, this is a paralyser'. Another theory as to the names is that a mob of cattle perished there when caught in a blizzard.

It's a popular destination for backcountry skiers.

The Paralyser from Blue Calf Mountain
I'd always been intrigued by some of the more unusual names bestowed upon the Snowy Mountain's peaks, with The Paralyser right up there with the best of them. It's part of the Perisher Range and can easily be viewed from many vantage points, with one of the best, as shown here, from the lookout near the Skitube terminal at Blue Calf. CL

Porcupine Rocks, so named because of their spiky like appearance. The rocks are easily reached from Perisher Valley and offer great views back towards Perisher and out across the vast Monaro Plains. Off to the west is Charlotte Pass and the Main Range while to the south there is a stunning vista along the Thredbo River Valley.

Footprints in the snow
The various sets of footprints I find when poking around in the snow country, whether it be native animals such as wombats, introduced ferals like deer and horses or the multitude of human marks from skis, snowshoes or boots, often leads me to wonder where have they been and where are they going? CL

MOUNT BLUE COW

VIEWS TO BLUE COW FROM GUTHEGA TRIG

During the 1840s Monaro grazier James Spencer imported a number of black English Shorthorn cattle which were crossed with white Shorthorns, the genetic mix producing calves with blue roan coats. Apparently one of these cross-bred cows would wander into the mountain lease after the thaw each year and, legend has it, that the beast would invariably be found on the mountain, which Spencer named Blue Cow.

With four snow resorts operating in the Perisher area and Charlotte Pass during the winter months, there are in excess of 50 lifts to transport downhill skiers, offering over 1250 ha of skiable terrain, ranging from the beginner friendly slopes

of Smiggin Holes to the more advanced runs at Perisher. Blue Cow offers day skiing while Guthega Resort is a relatively low key affair which can be accessed by road or from Blue Cow. Charlotte Pass, at 1765 metres, is the highest ski area in Australia. Access is by oversnow transport in winter as either a day trip or with overnight accommodation options. In summer, when the road between Perisher Valley and Charlotte Pass reopens, the area becomes the attention of walkers.

The Porcupine Rocks Track provides access for backcountry skiers and snowshoers to some great vantage points, high above the Perisher Valley. A popular circuit takes in Porcupine Rocks Track to Mount Duncan and Porcupine Rocks, where there are great views out across to Betts Camp, Charlotte Pass and the Main Range. The homeward route takes you below the summit of Mt Wheatley to Perisher Gap and back to Perisher Valley.

RIGHT: For those looking to escape the resort crowds there are over 100km of marked cross-country ski trails in and around the valley as well as a couple of dedicated snowshoe trails.

Backcountry adventurers have plenty of trails to explore, with a number of groomed routes radiating from the Perisher Nordic Shelter. These range from short 2.5km loops to longer 10km circuits. Marked trails are also available at Smiggin Holes and Mount Piper. Longer touring jaunts may be undertaken to Charlotte Pass via Trapyard Creek and Johnnies Plain while backcountry downhillers may like to explore the area around the Perisher Range and The Paralyser.

THE SNOWY RIVER
&
BEYOND

IMMORTALISED IN THE 1890 BANJO PATERSON POEM 'THE MAN FROM SNOWY RIVER'. THE 'SNOWY' STARTS ITS JOURNEY FROM HIGH UP IN THE ALPS AND IS JOINED BY CLUB LAKE CREEK AND BLUE LAKE CREEK, THEN BY SPENCERS CREEK AND POUNDS CREEK AS IT MAKES ITS WAY TO LAKE JINDABYNE. THE HIGHER REACHES ON THE SLOPES OF THE MAIN RANGE ARE OFTEN FROZEN OVER DURING THE WINTER MONTHS. ON ONE SIDE OF THE RIVER IS THE MAIN RANGE, DOMINATED HERE BY MOUNT TWYNAM AND MOUNT TATE WHILE OPPOSING IS THE PERISHER RANGE AND THE PARALYSER.

SNOWY RIVER

This once mighty watercourse is born on the eastern slopes of Mount Kosciuszko. Initially the fledgling stream meanders through a glaciated valley, carved out during the last ice age, as it makes its way to the first Snowy Mountains Scheme impoundment at Guthega.

Below its junction with Spencers Creek, the Snowy River bursts out into a picturesque valley which cuts between the Main Range and Perisher Range. This valley offers access to the northern part of the Main Range from Guthega. The 'Snowy' is crossed by a suspension footbridge near Illawong Lodge.

Looking across the junction of the Snowy River and Spencers Creek. Named after grazier and mountain guide James Spencer, the creek cuts through a gap between The Paralyser and Guthrie Ridge where it then joins with the Snowy River.

Originating under the brow of Mount Kosciuszko, The Snowy River flows through Kosciuszko and Alpine National Parks and the Snowy River National Park in Victoria before discharging into Bass Strait at Marlo. A short distance into its journey this once untamed river is captured by Guthega Pondage, the first Snowy Mountains Authority reservoir on the 'Snowy'.

SNOWY MOUNTAINS SCHEME

The Snowy Mountains Scheme consists of sixteen dams, seven power stations, a pumping station and 225 kilometres of tunnels, pipelines and aqueducts which diverts water captured in the high elevations of the Snowy Mountains into the westward flowing river systems of the Murray-Darling. Constructed between 1949 and 1974, the scheme is the largest engineering project so far undertaken in Australia. More than 100 000 people from over 30 countries were employed during the scheme's construction, including many immigrants fleeing war-ravaged Europe. Originally advanced to water the dry western inland, today, the scheme is the largest renewable energy generator on mainland Australia, supplying more than 65% of all renewable energy to the mainland market.

The ice encrusted waters of Guthega Pondage holds back flows from the upper reaches of the Snowy River, Guthega River, Spencers Creek and Pounds Creek. It was the first dam constructed as part of the Snowy Mountains Scheme and supplies water to Guthega Power Station.

Originally known as Pounds Creek Hut, this was one of the
first shelters built for recreational ski touring in the Snowy
Mountains back in the mid 1920s. In the mid 1950s it was
extended and became a private lodge, which it still functions
as today. Known as Illawong Lodge - Illawong meaning 'view
of the water' - the lodge sits on a small rise overlooking the
Snowy River, upstream of Guthega Village, with views out
across to Mount Twynam and Mount Tate and has the Perisher
Range as a backdrop.

GUTHEGA RIDGE

A SURREAL SNOWSCAPE

Guthega Trig looms large above, and to the north of, Guthega Pondage and the Snowy River. Here the charred skeletons of snow gums dance across the ridge, their ice fingers sparkling in the winter sun.

Looking towards Tate East Ridge from Guthega Trig
Tate East Ridge spears off the northern part of the Main Range, running in a southerly direction to the Snowy River. Its eastern flanks feed the Guthega River.

Survival

With the ground being covered in snow for
up to four months every year, alpine plants
and animals need to be hardy to survive in
the frigid landscape. But as winter retreats
and the snow becomes a distant memory,
the mountain herbfields burst into life with a
stunning array of colour.

BEYOND THREDBO

FOLLOW THE ALPINE WAY PAST THREDBO AND A WINTER WONDERLAND OF SNOW CLAD HILLS DOTTED WITH SNOW GUMS AND SECLUDED, STREAM-LINED VALLEYS AWAIT. AND THE BEST THING, IT'S ONLY A STONE'S THROW FROM THE FRENZY OF THREDBO'S DOWNHILL SLOPES. DEAD HORSE GAP IS THE SETTING OFF POINT FOR JOURNEYS UP AND ONTO THE HIGH GROUND OF THE SOUTH RAMS HEAD RANGE, WHILE TO THE SOUTH CASCADES TRAIL PROVIDES EASY ACCESS TO THE SHELTERED VALLEY OF THE UPPER REACHES OF THE THREDBO RIVER AND THE PILOT WILDERNESS.

CASCADES VALLEY

Apart from an information board and a small car parking area on the Alpine Way below Dead Horse Gap, there is little else to alert you to the delights of this tranquil valley where the upper reaches of the Thredbo River cut a swathe between rolling hills. Here you are on the edge of the vast Pilot Wilderness, its mountains and valleys stretching south to the Murray River.

A cloudless sky and frosty morning set the scene for my foray along the Cascades Trail. Strapping on my snowshoes at the trailhead, I followed beside the Thredbo River when it opened into a wide valley where this winter panorama spread out before me. CL

Snow gums dominate this sub-alpine landscape, being perfectly adapted to their unforgiving environment. Many of the trees here have been previously fire ravaged, but somehow this beauty has escaped past infernos, still standing tall and strong.

Fringed by snow gums for the first few kilometres, the Cascades Trail offers easy winter access from the Alpine Way near Dead Horse Gap. Here, as the sun commenced its daily journey across the sky, the snow, frozen by overnight frost, glistened radiantly.

Partially frozen by mid-winter's sub zero temperatures, the Thredbo River forms intricate patterns of ice, snow and water around a 'snow island'. Up until the 1970s the river was known as the Crackenback River, which I reckon is a much more evocative moniker. CL

- JAGUNGAL -
THE BIG BOGONG

REACHING TO A HEIGHT OF 2061 METRES, MOUNT JAGUNGAL STANDS SOLITARY ON A VAST HIGH COUNTRY PLAIN. DOMINATING THE LANDSCAPE, THE PEAK IS CLEARLY VISIBLE FOR MANY KILOMETRES IN ALL DIRECTIONS AND IS THE CROWNING JEWEL OF THE JAGUNGAL WILDERNESS AREA. ORIGINALLY KNOWN AS THE BIG BOGONG, IN SUMMER THE AREA OFFERS EXCELLENT WALKING AND CROSS-COUNTRY SKIING IN WINTER. MUCH OF THE WILDERNESS AREA IS MADE UP OF OPEN GRASSLAND, ROLLING HILLS AND MOUNTAIN STREAMS, WHICH MAKES FOR ENJOYABLE EXPLORATION, BOTH SUMMER AND WINTER.

MOUNT JAGUNGAL

Mount Jagungal is the dominant peak on Kosciuszko National Park's northern skyline and is also the most northern of the 2000 metre peaks. It came to the attention of the government surveyor Granville Stapylton in 1833 and originally named on his maps as the 'Big Bogong', a name also used by pioneering stockmen for the mountain. Jagungal is thought to be a derivative of an indigenous word relating to the bogong moth that migrates to the Alps each summer.

For those who make the trek, the summit of Mount Jagungal offers stupendous veiws in every direction. In both summer and winter it is a multi-day journey.

I'm always surprised, and often delighted by the many moods of Mount Jagungal. It somehow has a hold over me, a fascination which keeps drawing me back time and time again. To reach the summit, especially in winter, is quite an undertaking, but thankfully there are a number of vantage points where the 'sleeping lion' shows off its imposing stature. As if on cue, mother nature put on a fine twilight show from Mount Selwyn, bathing the sky in hues of pink and purple. CL

EXPLORING THE JAGUNGAL WILDERNESS

A sprawling wilderness in the north of Kosciuszko National Park with the brooding Mount Jagungal as its centrepiece, this is a place that invites serious exploration, but only by those who are well prepared. A spectacular sub-alpine environment, in summer most visitors access the area from the trailhead at Round Mountain, but come winter this route is restricted by the snow covered Tooma Road. At this time backcountry adventurers, either on skis or

LEFT: O'Keefes Hut sits proudly on the northern flank of Mount Jagungal and is a popular base for walkers to ascend the 'sleeping lion'. The hut was destroyed in the 2003 bushfires which razed Kosciuszko National Park, but was subsequently rebuilt in its original style.

snowshoes, come to the area from the south from Munyang at Guthega power station or from the east via Snowy Plain, which is by far the most direct route. Winter access from the north is from either Mount Selwyn or Kiandra via Table Top Mountain Trail. Even in the height of winter, snow cover may be marginal at lower elevations, so some walking is often required. For

A bushwalker trekking into the Jagungal Wilderness along Farm Ridge Trail. There are a number of access options for those wanting to tackle the mountain, which is clearly visable from all directions.

bushwalkers, the easiest summer access to the summit is from Grey Mare Trail, near where it crosses the Tumut River. Whichever way, or whichever season, it is a multi-day journey into the heart of this remote wilderness. While there are a number of huts in the region which are a boon when the weather turns rough, it is best not to rely on these for accommodation. The area, along with Gungartan, Brassy Mountains and The Kerries, is considered to offer some of the finest backcountry experiences in the mountains.

- THE NORTH -
MOUNT SELWYN & KIANDRA

SKIING BEGAN AT KIANDRA AROUND 1861, AND CONTINUED UNTIL THE MID 1970S. BUT A MORE RELIABLE SNOW COVER AT NEARBY MOUNT SELWYN SAW A PORTABLE ROPE TOW INSTALLED THERE IN 1966 AND BY 1978 KIANDRA'S REMAINING SKI FACILITIES HAD BEEN TRANSFERRED TO SELWYN. THIS INCLUDED AUSTRALIA'S FIRST T-BAR, WHICH HAD BEEN INSTALLED AT KIANDRA IN 1957. KIANDRA, APART FROM BEING THE SCENE OF ONE OF AUSTRALIA'S SHORTEST GOLD RUSHES, IS ALSO CREDITED WITH HAVING AUSTRALIA'S FIRST OFFICIAL SKI SLOPE AND HOLDING THE WORLDS FIRST SKIING COMPETITION.

MOUNT SELWYN

FUN IN THE SNOW

The family friendly Mount Selwyn Resort is ideal for those new to snowsports. The resort's gentle terrain is perfect for first timers while away from the resort there are some superb backcountry trips, including a number on marked trails.

Constructed by Chinese miners in 1882 to provide water for the sluicing operations at New Chum Hill at Kiandra, Three Mile Dam today is a popular recreation area in summer. Snowbound in winter, the surrounds can be explored on skis or snowshoes.

Along with Mount Jagungal, Table Top Mountain is a prominent landmark in the north of Kosciuszko National Park. At 1784 metres above sea level, the broad, flat summit sits comfortably in the rolling hills which were once fossicked by miners for gold.

KIANDRA

From the early 1860s gold was mined on the high plains near Kiandra. The goldfields had a population of about 10 000 people at its peak, and boasted at least 14 hotels, but the harsh winters and declining yields made the rush short lived. Kiandra is also credited as being the birthplace of downhill skiing in Australia, said to have been introduced by European miners. By the 1870s skiing was a common wintertime activity in the area. The last residents left in 1974 with Kiandra becoming a ghost town of dilapidated ruins and abandoned diggings.

Matthews Cottage, Kiandra
One of the few remaining buildings in the long deserted
ghost town, Matthews Cottage was built by the Foley family
sometime around 1906, well after mining activity had peaked.
The quaint weatherboard abode sits right beside the Snowy
Mountains Highway.

Scattered remnants offer a glimpse into the once busy Kiandra township. There is a short, signposted heritage walk with interpretive boards describing life in the settlement during its heyday. In addition to the township, there were a number of outlying diggings tucked away in the hills.

The harsh and often traumatic life of gold miners and their families is borne out here by this child's grave in the desolate, snow covered Kiandra Cemetery. A number of gravesites scattered across a tussocky hillside provides a stark reminder to just one of the many hardships faced for those who were part of Australia's shortest gold rush.

ALPINE AUSTRALIA

VICTORIA

MOUNT BOGONG
&
THE BOGONG HIGH PLAINS

LOOKING LIKE SOMETHING FROM A MEDIEVAL LEGEND, THE MOUNT BOGONG SUMMIT CAIRN SIGNALS TO BUSHWALKERS AND WINTER BACKCOUNTRY EXPLORERS THEY ARE STANDING ON TOP OF THE VICTORIAN ALPS AT 1986 METRES ABOVE SEA LEVEL. PART OF THE GREAT DIVIDING RANGE, MOUNT BOGONG AND THE NEARBY BOGONG HIGH PLAINS LAY WITHIN ALPINE NATIONAL PARK NEAR THE TOWN OF MOUNT BEAUTY. A UNIQUE WILDERNESS ENCOUNTER AWAITS EXPERIENCED BUSHWALKERS AND SKIERS WHO ARE DRAWN TO EXPLORE THE HUTS AND TRAILS OF THIS RUGGED AND UNFORGIVING LANDSCAPE.

MOUNT BOGONG

VICTORIA'S PINNACLE

At 1986 metres above sea level, Mount Bogong is the pinnacle of the Victorian Alps. When viewed from afar, it is easy to see why Victoria's highest mountain takes its name from the local aboriginal word for 'Big Fella'. Mount Bogong dominates the landscape, towering over the surrounding farmland and nearby township of Mount Beauty.

The Australian Alps have many moods and on this winter's afternoon it was particularly bleak, with low lying clouds shrouding Mount Bogong's famous summit from view. CM

Starting its journey near Falls Creek, Big River is fed by snow melt and run off from the northern reaches of Spion Kopje, which at 1841 metres is one of Victoria's ten highest mountains. As it meanders to the north and turns to the east, Big River dissects the landscape, carving a path between Mount Bogong and the High Plains.

With winter a distant memory and summer's warmth once again gracing the Victorian Alps, snow daisies and a host of wild flowers bloom across the slopes of Mount Bogong.

SPION KOPJE

PEAKS OF THE HIGH PLAINS

Views of Spion Kopje's rolling snow-capped summit greets visitors as they arrive at Falls Creek. Named from the Afrikaans meaning 'Spy Hill', it is common to see fresh tracks of more adventurous skiers exploring its slopes and the high plains after good dumps of snow.

ALPINE NATIONAL PARK

Established in 1989, Alpine National Park covers over 600 000 hectares stretching from Victoria's Central Gippsland to the edge of Kosciuszko National Park in New South Wales. Encompassing Victoria's highest peaks including Mount Bogong and Mount Feathertop, Alpine National Park protects a diverse landscape of mountain ash and snow gum woodlands, sweeping alpine meadows adorned by wildflowers in spring, plunging waterfalls and, in winter, its higher elevations disappearing beneath snow cover creating a majestic frozen wilderness.

The Crosscut Saw and Mount Howitt
After spending time in the high country above the snowline, Alpine Australia finds a special place in your heart. Whether you are enchanted by the snow gum woodlands, white capped summits or the never-ending views, visit once and you will find a reason to come back time and time again. CM

THE HIGH PLAINS

Set amidst Victoria's highest peaks, the Bogong High Plains like many of Australia's wilderness areas were once the domain of indigenous tribes and more recently European settlement, bushrangers and cattlemen. As the 19th and 20th centuries unfolded, the face of the landscape slowly changed. Rough-hewn bush huts appeared across the high plains in the 1800s while the 1900s saw the development of the Kiewa Valley Hydroelectric Scheme. When the weather closes in and the alpine grasses disappear beneath metres of snow, the Bogong High Plains radiate the wild essence of an inhospitable, windswept landscape.

As I wander the Bogong High Plains, there are days I feel the trails are limitless – I could explore them forever. CM

THE BOGONG HIGH PLAINS

LURE OF THE HIGH PLAINS

As I descended from heavy fog lingering atop Heathy Spur, dappled light danced across the rolling hills and windswept snow of the Bogong High Plains. The air was bitterly cold, yet as my eyes followed the meandering cross-country trail of Heathy Spur Loop, I could see skiers in the distance happily exploring, even as heavy snow was promising to fall. CM

Snow from a recent cold front lingers on the horizon, its melt feeding the crystal clear alpine streams which flow across the Bogong High Plains. Burbling gently, these high country streams can be heard from afar as they meander over beds of smooth river rocks, polished by their passing.

I love the unpredictable nature of the Bogong High Plains, grey overcast days fade as late afternoon light washes across the sweeping plains bathing sky and land in golden hues. CM

WALLACE'S HUT

Over 100 years have now passed since the Wallace brothers built this lonely little hut on the Bogong High Plains. Hidden from view, amongst a spectacular grove of gnarled and stunted snow gums, it provided shelter for the Wallace family during the spring and summer months, as their cattle grazed on the sweet grasses of the alpine meadows.

A survivor of bushfires and raging blizzards, Wallace's Hut is now the oldest surviving hut of the Victorian high country, and a national treasure. Its enchanted setting offers stark contrast to the adjacent vast Bogong High Plains.

FALLS CREEK

Falls Creek rests on the edge of the Bogong High Plains and Rocky Valley Lake, its village nestled amongst woodlands of snow gums at 1600 metres. Only 45 minutes from Mount Beauty, Falls Creek offers 14 lifts for downhill skiing and 65km of extensive cross-country trails stretching out into the Bogong High Plains. With its first lodge built in 1948 and lift in 1951, Falls Creek now caters for 5000 overnight visitors with ski in and out accommodation.

Rocky Valley Lake - Falls Creek
I love mountain sunsets which erupt unexpectedly at the end of an otherwise cold, bleak afternoon. They begin with only a hint of colour as the sun slips through a small break amongst the clouds, ending with a rush as the last rays of sunlight dance across the sky, lingering for a moment before night slowly settles across the Alps. CM

ROCKY VALLEY

SHADOWS OF WINTER

Idyllically set on the Bogong High Plains, Rocky Valley Lake was created for the Kiewa Hydroelectric Scheme in the mid 1900s. Surrounded by rolling hills covered in snow gums, Rocky Valley Lake freezes over during particularly cold winters and is at its most beautiful when the skies are dark with low hanging clouds and the wind blowing snow across its icy surface.

MOUNT HOTHAM
&
BEYOND

SET HIGH ABOVE THE SNOWLINE AMIDST THE RUGGED PEAKS AND VALLEYS OF THE GREAT DIVIDING RANGE, MOUNT HOTHAM IS HOME TO THE HIGHEST ALPINE VILLAGE IN AUSTRALIA. ONLY FOUR AND A HALF HOURS DRIVE FROM MELBOURNE, MOUNT HOTHAM IS A GATEWAY TO EXCELLENT SKIING AND WALKING. BEYOND THE MOUNTAIN BACKCOUNTRY ADVENTURE CAN BE FOUND ON THE PLAINS EXPLORING SNOW GUM WOODLANDS, OR BY CROSSING THE ALPINE WILDERNESS TO MOUNT FEATHERTOP OR FALLS CREEK.

MOUNT HOTHAM

The old saying 'the journey is as important as the destination' certainly rings true when travelling to Mount Hotham. The road to the mountain twists and bends as it snakes its way around the ranges to climb to Mount Hotham at 1861 metres. Once arriving on Mount Hotham spectacular sweeping views across the surrounding plains and valleys to distant peaks can be taken in.

Shrouded amidst fog during winter storms, Mount Hotham's views, can at times, be elusive. In the moments however, when the fog passes and a glimpse into the valleys below are to be had, the time spent waiting on nature is rewarded.

Set to the south-west of Mount Hotham and part of the Great Dividing Range, The Twins distinctive peaks stand out against the Barry Mountains Range. At 1680 metres they cast a long shadow over the valleys below against the splendour of the setting sun.

Even in winter the impact of past alpine fires can be seen across the mountains. Winter ice covers the scarred burnt limbs of snow gum woodlands.

I love the drama of winter. Low laying clouds drift across the sky, as light and fog frolic across the frozen shapes and forms of the landscape. CM

MOUNT FEATHERTOP

VIEW TO FEATHERTOP FROM MOUNT HOTHAM

With its windswept peak rising to an elevation of 1922 metres above sea level, Mount Feathertop rests on the roof of Victoria as the state's second highest mountain. Spectacular throughout the year, the view across Mount Feathertop is particularly stunning during the winter months, as temperatures plummet and snowfalls transform the landscape into a winter wonderland.

DINNER PLAIN

As the Great Alpine Road passes over Mount Hotham and begins its descent towards Omeo, the landscape changes dramatically. The great peaks and sheer drop off on the northern Harrietville approach give way to high plains, their rolling meadows covered in snow gum woodlands. Once on the eastern side of Mount Hotham and the village, the road passes through JB Plain. Those with a keen eye can catch glimpses, through the trees, of a small red hut almost hidden from view, before arriving at Dinner Plain. Idyllically surrounded by the Alpine National Park, the Dinner Plain Village has a distinctive charm. Its architect inspired by High Country cattlemen's huts of a bygone era. With a beginners ski slope and a network of walking trails stretching back towards Mount Hotham, the Village offers a great opportunity to explore Dinner Plain and its surrounds.

Come winter, I love to strap on snowshoes and explore the plains below Mount Hotham, wandering amongst snow gum woodlands and watching as winter slowly envelops. CM

Nestled peacefully amongst snow gum woodland on the rolling incline of JB Plain, a rustic little hut lures visitors. Travellers on the plain can retreat to the hut from the bitter chill of a frozen alpine evening and warm themselves inside beside a roaring fire.

As another snow storm passes in a particularly good winter, the alpine grasses of Dinner Plain slowly disappear under an ever thickening blanket of white.

CRB HUT

ON DINNER PLAIN

Standing across from the entrance of the Dinner Plain Village, CRB Hut with its rough charm blends quietly into a landscape shrouded in snow and fog. Built by the Country Roads Board around 1923, it was one of several which provided refuge for those workers on the road upgrade between Harrietville and Omeo.

THE
MOUNT BUFFALO
PLATEAU

KNOWN AS THE 'ISLAND IN THE SKY', MOUNT BUFFALO RISES DRAMATICALLY ABOVE THE VALLEYS BELOW. IT'S IMPOSING GRANITE ESCARPMENTS, LIKE ANCIENT BATTLEMENTS, PROTECTING A PLATEAU OF REMARKABLE BEAUTY. A LANDSCAPE OF ALPINE MEADOWS, GNARLED SNOW GUMS, WATERFALLS AND TOWERING GRANITE TORS, THE PLATEAU HAS HELD A SPECIAL PLACE IN THE HEART OF EXPLORERS AND NATURE LOVERS SINCE THE 1800S.

The Mount Buffalo Plateau is often a scene of contradictions. A landscape ravaged by summer fires, becomes a winter wonderland as heavy snow dumps across the Victorian Alps. The snow gum's burnt scars disappear under a cover of snow and ice come winter.

As cold weather descends across the southern states in late autumn, many trees in the Victorian Alps shed long strands of bark, creating unique patterns in their trunks. With snow falling in winter, the wet conditions intensify the colours in the trunks creating a beautiful contrast to the snow's starkness.

MOUNT BUFFALO PLATEAU

VIEWS FROM THE HORN

Late in the afternoon as the sun dips low in the sky and the last light of day dances across the landscape, Mount Buffalo's Horn offers a unique perspective of the plateau. At an elevation of 1723m, The Horn is the highest point on the mountain and on a clear day, you can enjoy breathtaking 360-degree views.

MOUNT BUFFALO
NATIONAL PARK

A short drive from the township of Bright, Mount Buffalo National Park had humble beginnings, with 1165 hectares around Eurobin Falls first reserved as a National Park in 1898. Today as one of Victoria's oldest parks it covers most of the mountain, protecting an area of 31 000 hectares, rising to a peak of 1723 metres at The Horn. The national park covers a diverse landscape of sub-alpine vegetation, where, if you are lucky you may see wombats, wallabies or the occasional alpine dingo.

The Keep on Le Souef Plateau - Mount Buffalo National Park Snow had fallen heavily across the plateau over the course of the afternoon. As the storm passed the snow laden peaks momentarily emerged from their foggy shroud–tranquility settled across the landscape. Moments later, the sun slipped away and the day faded to night. As a photographer, I never tire of moments like these. CM

THE CATHEDRAL

Towering high above the meadows of the Mount Buffalo Plateau, The Cathedral overlooks a spectacular sub-alpine wilderness. A lonely and often inhospitable environment, the plateau bears the scars of the harsh winters and summer wildfires that have shaped the mountain's character over the ages.

It was a cold autumn's afternoon as I meandered amongst the rocks and twisted snow gums, past The Cathedral and on towards The Hump. As I continued to climb, the track eventually emerged from amongst the trees, offering sweeping views of The Cathedral and surrounding landscape. CM

I have been fascinated by this tree for many years and as I survey its gnarled form, shaped by a lifetime in extreme conditions, I am reminded that in nature true beauty often lies in the imperfections. CM

THE CHALET

With the Victorian government recognising the tourism potential of Mount Buffalo, a chalet was built overlooking the towering escarpment walls of Bents Lookout in 1910. Reflecting an opulence of a bygone era, the chalet has become a beloved feature of the mountain with visitors regularly pausing to admire its beautiful gardens. Recognised for '...architectural, historical and social significance' the chalet is listed in the Victorian Heritage Register.

THE GAP

BUFFALO'S TRANSFORMING LANDSCAPES

During the summer months, many will drive pass this scene on their way to the chalet or Horn with little thought of stopping to admire its beautiful, muted tones of alpine grasses, rocks and snow gums. Winter snowfalls however, bring with them a touch of magic that can transform the landscape and our perception of it in moments.

The Gorge
As the sun disappeared below the horizon and
the last of its warmth lingered for a moment,
the view across the gorge to the distant hills
was one to savour.

Snow in Sun
The Alps are beautiful and unpredictable. One moment it is bitterly cold with snow falling heavily and next minute, the sun breaks through bringing a touch of welcome warmth.

EXPLORING MOUNT BUFFALO NATIONAL PARK

A mountain of beautiful alpine meadows, sheer cliffs and plunging waterfalls, Mount Buffalo is not only one of the state's most spectacular national parks, but also one of its oldest. However, long before European explorers passed through the mountain landscape Aboriginal tribes would ascend the ranges during the summer months to escape the heat of the plains. Here they held corroborees and initiations, socialised and feasted on the protein rich bogong moths.

LEFT: On a cold winter's afternoon, a weathered stone shelter, its ageing shingles laden with snow, blends peacefully into the landscape.

William Hovel and Hamilton Hume were the first Europeans to view the mountain and the plateau during their 1824 exploration from Sydney to Port Phillip Bay. Eyeing the mountain from a distance, they remarked that its likeness was that of a sleeping buffalo, thus giving the mountain its name. It was not long before this ancient mountain was visited by gold miners,

Eurobin Creek burbles joyfully as it flows over a cascade of mossy boulders, amidst the ferns and gums of the lower slopes of Mount Buffalo. Reduced to a trickle during the summer months, Eurobin Creek comes to life over winter, as increased rainfall and melting snow run into the network of creeks and streams that cross the mountain.

cattlemen and botanists. Tourism was pioneered by James and John Manfield when they guided their first tourist party onto the plateau in 1865.

Isolated high above the surrounding landscape and with only the lightest human touch, early tourists entered an unspoilt mountain paradise created by turbulent volcanic forces and shaped over eons by ice, wildfire, rain and wind. One can only imagine their reaction, having crossed the sweeping alpine meadows of the plateau as they encountered the towering escarpment walls of Mount Buffalo Gorge.

MOUNT BULLER
&
MOUNT STIRLING

SET SIDE BY SIDE AND A LITTLE OVER THREE HOURS DRIVE FROM MELBOURNE, MOUNT BULLER AND MOUNT STIRLING ARE A TALE OF TWO MOUNTAINS, OFFERING VASTLY DIFFERENT ALPINE EXPERIENCES TO THEIR VISITORS. MOUNT BULLER IS A VIBRANT, DOWNHILL RESORT WITH 22 LIFTS COVERING 300 HECTARES; WHILE MOUNT STIRLING CATERS TO THOSE SEEKING A BACKCOUNTRY EXPERIENCE SUCH AS CROSS-COUNTRY SKIING, SNOWSHOEING, SNOW CAMPING, AND SNOWBOARDING STANLEY BOWL NEAR THE SUMMIT.

Sunset explodes over the Mt Buller ridgeline

MOUNT
BULLER
VILLAGE

Set amongst the rolling slopes of Mount Buller, the village, at 1600 metres, began with the construction of a chalet in 1929. Until the first ski lift opened in 1949, skiing was a far more arduous sport with visitors walking to the top of the runs before skiing down. Today, with three terrain parks, 22 lifts covering 300 hectares of ski fields and an accommodation capacity of 7000 beds, Mount Buller has grown to become Victoria's largest ski resort.

The Village - Mount Buller
As Mount Buller's ski lifts stop turning and the day slowly fades, the lights of the village stand out against the approaching darkness. Perched high above, I watch as visitors retreat from the cold into the warmth of the mountains' bars, restaurants and accommodation, while the more adventurous, ignoring the temperatures, pass by me braving an evening jog! CM

MOUNT BULLER

THE SUMMIT

Of Mount Buller's 22 ski lifts, two deposit skiers just below the mountain's summit of 1805m. From this vantage point skiers are offered spectacular views on bluebird days as they disconnect from the world for a moment before putting their abilities to the test along a choice of intermediate and advanced runs.

Mount Buller Sunset
Although fog had swept across the Alps late in the afternoon,
Mount Buller emerged at nightfall, its distinctive form set
against the backdrop of a spectacular sunset.

Unique snow patterns form on Mount Buller's summit during the constant cycle of softening during the day and refreezing at night; and at times buffeted by strong winds.

At an elevation of 1725 metres, The Bluff's distinctive plateau is often adorned by winter snow. Located within Alpine National Park, The Bluff lies across the Howqua Valley to the south of Mount Buller.

SNOW SPORTS

As the Queen's Birthday heralds the beginning of another ski season, Victoria's Alps become a playground for downhill and cross-country skiers, snowboarders and those exploring the backcountry on snowshoes.

MOUNT STIRLING SUMMIT

Mount Stirling, named after James Stirling who surveyed the Victorian Alps, is a short drive from Mansfield and in close proximity to Mount Buller. Covering an area of 3000 hectares, Mount Stirling Ski Resort offers a toboggan run for families at Telephone Box Junction along with 68km of cross-country trails and snowboarding at Stanley Bowl near the summit of 1749 metres. For those seeking a true backcountry experience, overnight camping is encouraged and is a great opportunity to explore the mountain to its fullest.

Mount Stirling from Mount Buller
From a young age, I have had a love for the grandeur and drama of the Victorian Alps. There are few moments in life which are as peaceful as sitting high above the valleys below and watching the last rays of sweet red light wash across distant snow-capped peaks. CM

MOUNT STIRLING

SWEEPING VISTAS

The Mount Stirling backcountry has a wonderful sense of isolation during the winter months. There are few crowds and the only way to explore the mountain is by foot, with many taking the opportunity to camp in the snow under the stars. For those who visit the summit, sweeping views of snow-capped Mount Speculation and the Crosscut Saw await.

Believed to be over 300 years old, the Mount Stirling summit tree, as it is affectionately known, stands alone, the only tree to grow on the mountain's 23 hectare summit. A well-loved feature of the mountain, many visit the summit just to see this grand old snow gum.

Same snow gum, different season. It is remarkable to consider the Mount Stirling summit tree has survived over 300 winters, isolated upon Mount Stirling and was at least 117 years of age at the founding of Melbourne in 1835.

EXPLORING MOUNT STIRLING

W ith its close proximity to Melbourne, Mount Stirling is a popular destination throughout the year for nature lovers of all persuasions. The cool summer air, distant mountain views and kilometres of trails draw bushwalkers, mountain bikers and those exploring by four-wheel drive; with the nearby Craig's Hut one of the main drawcards. In winter, fresh snowfalls call to those who love exploring backcountry snow gum woodlands, windswept peaks or skiing an untamed mountain summit.

LEFT: Marking the highest point on the Mount Stirling summit, the trig point is clearly visible from Mount Buller and played an important role in early surveys of the Victorian Alps.

Free from development, save for a small, low key visitor centre at Telephone Box Junction and a handful of refuge huts, the Mount Stirling backcountry has a wonderful sense of isolation during the winter months. There are few crowds and the only way to explore the mountain is by foot, with many taking the opportunity to sleep in the comfort of Bluff

On a clear day, the views from Mount Stirling across Alpine National Park are nothing short of breathtaking. Recent snowfalls highlight the distant peaks, with the rugged outline of the Crosscut Saw clearly visible.

Spur Hut or snow camping under the stars. On the lower reaches of Mount Stirling there are sheltered snow gum woodlands and stands of alpine ash to explore. From the summit, sweeping views across Alpine National Park await. Although there are no ski lifts, Stanley and Dugout Bowls, close to the summit, offer excellent skiing after good snowfalls. With 68kms of trails, well prepared cross-country skiers and snowshoers can stay out for days, soaking up the majesty of the backcountry.

IMAGE INDEX

NEW SOUTH WALES

THROUGH THE LENS

Unlike many photographers, I didn't take up the craft at an early age and came to photography in my late 20's. Much has changed in the time since I received my Canon EOS 500n as a Christmas present from my family. Although I still like film, I love the way that digital allows me to capture the bright snow and dark valleys of the mountains.

I developed a love for the Victorian Alps in my early years and hold dear the memories of holidays spent in Bright, nestled in the foothills near Mount Buffalo, Falls Creek and Hotham. I remember building dams in the Ovens River with dad, watching sunrise with mum and encountering my first snow on Mount Buffalo. As I explore the Alps as a photographer, I can see fleeting shadows of my childhood self, set against the rugged landscape.

As I consider my journey over the years, and particularly the last few months photographing the Victorian Alps for *Alpine Australia*, I am reminded that it is not enough to simply love taking photographs if we want to capture the spirit of this extreme landscape. When the temperature drops below freezing, a biting wind cuts to the bone and fog shrouds the very view you are attempting to photograph, it takes a love for the alpine landscape with a healthy dose of passion.

I am often inspired by the words of the great Tasmanian photographer Peter Dombrovskis who once said, 'When you go out there, you don't get away from it all. You get back to it all. You come home to what's important. You come home to yourself'. While not everybody can visit the Australian Alps, I hope my photography can in some small part capture the essence of its spirit for others to experience.

There is however, so much more to the story of the photographs in *Alpine Australia* than pretty images on a page. It includes the people I have met along the way, the spirit of the locations and the occasional mishap which strikes at unexpected moments. A few of which I would like to share here.

I have to confess, I almost missed one of my favourite photographs in the book (page 188-189). It was late in the afternoon and as fog brought a white-out to Mount Buller, I held little hope for a colourful sunset. For a moment I even considered cutting my losses and indulging in an early dinner. With no warning, the fog thinned a little and I decided to head out across the snow in case something was to happen. With the slopes icy and sunset beginning to glow, I found myself stuck on a slippery incline sliding backwards. As I sat there fighting to fasten my snow-shoes, I watched as sunset unfolded. With the snow-shoes finally on, I sprinted with the grace of a wombat across the snow, setting up the camera and capturing the moment just as the light began to fade.

The Mount Stirling summit snow gum (Page 199) is an icon on the mountain, being a must see sight for anybody visiting the area. As I was photographing, I witnessed a beautiful moment when a family arrived pulling a sled with a snowman on it. The children then carefully placed the snowman behind the tree, so it could live for ever.

I had been chasing a sunset photograph of Mount Feathertop (Page 152-153) for years, only to leave empty handed courtesy of fog, strong winds or lack of snow. Finally after a period of good snowfall and promising weather I returned. A gentle breeze swirled across the mountain, while scattered cloud drifted slowly overhead. As the last red rays of sunlight danced off the clouds and across the mountains I finally had my shot. Some photographs are years in the making but take only moments to capture.

Time in the field can be challenging. In photographing the Alps there is mud to navigate, ice to cross, numb toes, inhospitable weather and wildlife to contend with. Usually I am well prepared for all of these, however on a particularly cold night on Mount Stirling with the temperature dropping to minus 5 and a minus 14 wind chill, I woke to find my water bottle had leaked in the tent; soaking my one and only pair of gloves. My attempt to dry the gloves using my stove was almost a mistake as I watched flames jumping from the fingers! Note to self, remember to take a second pair of gloves.

- Chris Munn -

To see more of Chris' extensive Australia wide image portfolio and limited edition prints visit
www.chrismunngallery.com

Craig Lewis is the author and photographer of numerous Australiana books, including perennial favourites *Australian Bush Pubs* and *High Country Huts and Homesteads*. He has travelled extensively throughout Australia; camping out, photographing and writing about his adventures for the past 20 or so years. He lives in the New South Wales High Country.

You can follow Craig's work on instagram @boilingbillyimages

Chris Munn is a photographer based in Yackandandah at the foothills of the Victorian High Country. His love for the Victorian Alps began at an early age, with family trips to Mount Buffalo and the Bogong High Plains. He has been exploring and photographing this spectacular region for the past 14 years, capturing its magnificent vistas in all seasons. *Alpine Australia* is his first book.

More of Chris's work can be found at **www.chrismunngallery.com**

BOILING BILLY

A licensed imprint to Woodslane Press
10 Apollo Street, Warriewood NSW 2102 Australia
Email: info@woodslane.com.au
Tel: 02 8445 2300
www.woodslane.com.au

This hardcover edition first published in 2018

Copyright © text Craig Lewis and Chris Munn 2018
Copyright © Photographs Craig Lewis | Boiling Billy Images 2018
Copyright © Photographs Chris Munn | Chris Munn Photography 2018

Respect copyright, encourage creativity

Book design and layout: Craig Lewis | Boiling Billy Publications
Editing and proofreading: Cathy Savage | Boiling Billy Publications

Printed in China by Asia Pacific Offset

ISBN: 9781921874864

A catalogue record for this
book is available from the
National Library of Australia

Boiling Billy Publications welcomes feedback from readers. If you would like to get in touch then please write or e-mail us at:
Boiling Billy Publications, Nimmitabel NSW 2631
E-mail: info@boilingbilly.com.au
Web: www.boilingbilly.com.au
www.facebook.com/boilingbilly
Tel: 02 6454 6162

Also from the publisher:

High Country Huts and Homesteads - A Celebration of Australia's Mountain Shelters
by Craig Lewis and Cathy Savage
ISBN: 9781925403398
RRP: $49.99